NEW &
SELECTED
poems

Also By Anthony S. Abbott

POETRY
The Girl in the Yellow Raincoat
A Small Thing Like A Breath
The Search For Wonder
        In The Cradle of the World
The Man Who

FICTION
Leaving Maggie Hope
The Three Great Secret Things

NEW & SELECTED

poems

1989 – 2009

ANTHONY S. ABBOTT

LORIMER PRESS

DAVIDSON, NC

2009

ACKNOWLEDGEMENTS

The Charlotte Observer, "Something Simple"
Journey Without: The Charlotte Writers Club Anthology, Vol. 4, "Blood Red of
    Late October"
The Davidson Journal, "The Girl"
Iodine, "On the Day the Ashes Fell in Pompeii" and "Home Is"
The Poetry Council of NC, "After Vespers"

St. Andrews College Press, *The Girl in the Yellow Raincoat*, *A Small Thing Like
a Breath*, and *The Search for Wonder in the Cradle of the World*

Main Street Rag Publishing Company, *The Man Who*

Published in the United States
Lorimer Press, Davidson, North Carolina.

Book Design - Leslie Rindoks
Cover Photo - Gansovsky Vladislav

Library of Congress Control Number: 2009936258

ISBN 978-0-9789342-7-9

For Lynnie

There are days we live
as if death were nowhere
in the background, from joy
to joy to joy, from wing to wing,
from blossom to blossom to
impossible blossom, to sweet impossible blossom.

–Li-Young Lee

Contents

Foreword
by
Fred Chappell

Of all the world's craftsmen, few will be so distrustful of his tools as the poet. If the carpenter believed that his saw would produce a ragged cut, he would discard it; if the plumber knew that his flange would result in an imperfect connection, he would cut it off. But the poet is forced to use words and these can only approximate or suggest or pallidly echo what is in their user's mind and heart.

Anthony Abbott is a celebrated, widely published, and warmly appreciated poet. If critical notice fulfilled artistic ambitions, he should be content. But here are the opening stanzas of "The Man Who Speaks to His Daughter on Her 40th Birthday":

"Poetry is the supreme fiction," says Wallace Stevens.
I know. Then how to express the truth, simple
and unadorned as Stevens's "dresser of deal."

You see, I am already equivocating, ducking
behind the decoration of language. So, stop me.
Good. That's better. Now, tell me where you are.

His plan here is to disarm, to charm us by admitting to the inadequacy of the means at his disposal for expressing "the truth." Yet his chagrin is genuine; words will not perform the task he demands of them. But they are the only things he has got.

I think that even the very best of our lyric poets—W. B. Yeats, say, or Robert Herrick or Thomas Hardy—might look at a newly completed poem with some sense of satisfaction. "That is not so bad," he might say—and then, shaking his head glumly—"but it is not what I set out to write."

Two of Abbott's poems, "Stirring the Muse" and "Words Are the Only Fingers of the Soul," address this concern with the shortcomings of his metier directly and at some length. In the latter, he finds a wonderful image for making visible the invisible, for making tangible the intangible, for demonstrating how the most seemingly powerless things in the world change and tinge the world:

> Words are the only fingers of the soul
> words spoken and heard
> written and received
>
> like hands thrust deep into bowls
> of ripe cherries, then pulled,
> burgundy stained, into the air.

A profound artistic skepticism underlies all the pieces in *New and Selected Poems: 1989-2009*. That is a surprising thing to say of a volume so full of variety, so redolent with reminiscence, so urgent with love, so colorful with imagery, and so affirmative with statement. There is nothing drab or coy here; Abbott's world is alive, chirping and talking, singing and thinking. But his is a world that thought pervades and in which the intense awareness of the poet often turns to the craft with all its attendant conundrums and ambiguities. What is the goal of art, this volume asks, and though the poet may have to consent to the idea that art is its own end as well as its means, he is not satisfied with it.

Even so, he will forgive himself his moments of impatience ("I got nothing but goddam words working for me," "Blood Talk" says) because he cannot dispossess himself of the urge, the need, and the duty to express what he so momentously feels: "I turn the dazzle inward / and down. It courses through the veins / and lofts me toward the breathless light." ("Blood Red of Late October")

It cannot be said of all good poetry that it finally strives toward the condition of silence. Chaucer, for instance, is a great poet who has no stake in silence. But for many a serious, deep-bowed poet, a thoughtful silence may be the last, finest epitome of what he strives to say and to mean:

The Man Who Feels the Sleeves of the Snow

On the day after the snow
he takes his usual walk.
The trees
reach out to him.
Their silver sleeves
have no history
no memory of grief.
Their long white fingers know only
the sweet silence
of snow.

NEW POEMS

2009

Something Simple

The need to write something
simple and unadorned like
a bride at a Quaker wedding
or a single candle or the
full moon on a winter night

to say something unequivocal
like I love you, or, it rained
last night. I have been lost
for so long that the trick
has quite eluded me.

No Country for Old Men

"That is no country for old men. The young
In one another's arms, birds in the trees
—Those dying generations—at their song"
　　　　　—W. B. Yeats, "Sailing to Byzantium"

True enough. I count the steps at our
Paris Metro stop. Sixty-nine if I am right.
I pause at thirty-two to breathe, grasp
the banister and pull myself up.

Old men don't ride the metro. They are
all in the parks playing Bocci or whatever
the French call it. They wear berets, smoke
cigarettes, move as one smooth unit,

and there are no old women in Paris
at least none that I can see, walking
their dogs down the street or sitting in the
narrow Metro seats. The women are beautiful

and thin, they all look like lovers.
Yeats himself came to Paris as a young
man in search of Maude Gonne,
his whole life a lament for her loss.

His ghost haunts me now, as I stare
stupidly at the banks from the bow
of the tour boat, looking, looking
for something I cannot name.

The Girl

Advanced poetry class. Students around
a table, the girl at the end, thinking
with the tip of her pen between her teeth.
I loved her poems, her slightly sensual,

off-beat love poems, with just a twist
of irony. One November afternoon
she read a new one, a step beyond.
"It's beautiful," I said. The class agreed.

Trouble was, it wasn't hers. Another
student found the text and brought it
to my office door. The copy burned
in my hand. This could not be, I said.

She was good. Good enough to hold us all
with her own words. No need for this.
I paused, but had no choice. At the trial
her parents glared at me. They thought

I had betrayed her. Before she left,
she came to me and said she could not
bear it if I hated her. "Come back," I said,
"and we will start again. I believe in you."

Two years later, exile served, she wrote
once more, better than ever. She and the four
others in the new class road-tripped with me,
told stories, laughed, recited poems together

behind the slight headlights of the car.
I still hear from her at Christmas. Yesterday
a card came with a picture of her daughter,
a four-year old with her mother's pensive smile.

Madonna, Thinking

Reflections on Piero della Francesca's
"Madonna del Parto"

On a summer afternoon, during
siesta time, the town is quiet
except for the buses which bring tourists
to see the painting, now cleaned, restored

and hung in an old school. Get there early
if you can. The fewer people the better.
Alone you can look at the Madonna's face
for a long, long time. You might be struck

first by the blue of her dress or the left
hand on the hip, the right supporting
her child. Yes, these are lovely things
but it is her face which will hold you.

You can't divine her thoughts from her
expression, but you try. You study
her lips, curved down in sadness, her deep
brown eyes, the right almost closed,

the left speaking of something she has felt,
pain perhaps, or knowledge of who she bears,
or doubt that she is worthy of this task.
I don't know. She's very Tuscan, very

real, very strong. Her body will have no
trouble with this birth. She's in charge now
and always was. Still the grief of the ages
and all the knowledge, too, are on her face.

She knows the price, and agreed to pay
when she told the angel yes in another
quiet town during siesta time on a
summer afternoon.

Blood Red of Late October

Blood red of late October in the South,
and from the cemetery to the college campus
on the hill, the leaves bathe my eyes. I
turn each corner into dazzling surprise.

In my mind's eye, she walks toward me.
I show her my favorite tree. I pluck three
leaves for her and watch as she carries
them away. This is new found grace,

and in the space where sadness once lay
the small white flower of hope grows.
In the South, October lingers, the gold
sun glances off the trees. November will

come with its cold rain soon enough,
I know. I turn the dazzle inward
and down. It courses through the veins
and lofts me toward the breathless light.

On The Day The Ashes Fell In Pompeii

workers left their tools behind and ran.
Horses were closed in the barns.

One man lay down in his garden
only inches from his gate, clutching

a brass key. Mothers covered their babies
with their bodies. A dog lay curled under

a bed. When the bodies were recovered
centuries later, they had been preserved,

forever, in the exact positions of their deaths,
some clutching bags or boxes of jewels

they thought might save them in the days ahead.
The lovers clutched only each other.

When the ash solidified and flesh decayed
a perfect space was formed, leaving

an absolute impression even of facial
features. It haunts me still, the way

the bodies seem to live again when we
pass them on the rebuilt streets and gaze

into their rooms. The guides do not
need to speak. We stop and look and feel

the sudden sting of cold. You too, they seem
to say. Overheard the mountain seeps steam.

"Tout Fini"

The man who had once lived
    walked the city streets
        in the early morning

He passed runners
    their muscled legs
        bare in the winter air

and he passed yellow vans
    delivering their hot
        pastries to bakeries.

He passed what must
    have been the local
        bartenders hurrying home.

All around the city,
    shifts were changing,
        trains were filling,

lovers waking,
    still wrapped
        in each other's limbs.

From a bench in Washington Square
    he watched two
        small dachshunds

in red coats
    being walked
        by a woman

all in black
    with a Russian hat.
        He remembered a girl

her face in the partly opened door
    her damp hair curled on her neck
        her eyes looking up—a long time ago.

The man who had once lived
    knew it was "tout fini"
        as the French say.

His feet were cold.
    "Well," he said to his toes.
        "At least I shall have new shoes."

After Vespers

you were kneeling
on the stone floor
of the stone church

your elbows propped
on the wooden rail
your eyes closed

in prayer. I came
to you and knelt.
You did not look up

but you knew I was there.
We did not need to speak.
I know the words

of your prayers and you
know mine. Silence
held us. Light shifted.

The smell of incense
and candles lingered
from vespers.

All the others had
departed. Only the red
light of the sacrament

still burned and the streetlight
beyond the open door
where I waited yesterday

and the day before.

New York City—In The Subway, 2008

I leave the train at Chambers Street and follow
the sound of grunting steam shovels to Ground
Zero. Nothing there, absolutely nothing
to help us remember the dead, nothing but
orange dinosaur cranes lifting and sifting dirt.

Then I see the slim steeple of St. Paul's Chapel.
Inside, hundreds—young and old, black and tan
and white—file in silence by the photographs
and drawings, small tokens of life
from those who felt the black cloud.

Over the altar a banner from the people
of Oklahoma filled with the simple words
of children, thanking the firemen and the cops,
the hard hatted workers who dug so deep
to save what could be saved. Later, I take

the D train to Coney Island and walk the long
boardwalk. It all looks so tired. Maybe I
should not have come. I take the N train back
to Manhattan. As we rise into the open
air and cross the East River, the sun is setting

over the Statue of Liberty. The Brooklyn Bridge
glows like a talisman. Sparks of illumination
climb from the water, upward to the tall buildings,
hanging there, momentarily, before the train
slides once more into darkness.

Home Is

Sometimes at night
on the back lanes
I cannot feel my own steps

and the silence wears
a comforting cloak.
Is heaven like that?

Rooms full of nameless voices
I have known before
in awkward guesses?

I only know that I know
less than before. They say
I should empty out

but now that emptying
is just another kind of sleep
not the deep opening

I need. I think the very leaves
would sound like home
if only I could hear them

and that one star over
my head might look
like home if only I could

hold it in my arms
before it dissolved
into day.

FROM
THE GIRL IN THE YELLOW RAINCOAT

1989

The Girl in the Yellow Raincoat

waits on the sidewalk outside
my window. The flower in her hair
is wet. She stands very still

her eyes focused upward on some
object I cannot see. She does not
move, but she smiles…slightly.

Perhaps she plays the cello
and she is humming Bartok silently
making the bow ripple with her tongue

against her teeth. Or, maybe, she waits
for a bus to take her to her lover.
Or she has read a letter from Paris

or Istanbul and she smells coffee
and chestnuts steam roasted and she
hears in the cobbled streets the cries

of vendors under the aged curves
of bridges. Perhaps she is just a girl
standing in the rain by a stone bench

in the early morning while the
street shines. It is nothing—you argue.
Then why do I weep, and why are there

splinters in my palms, and why do I
stand here, long, long, after she is
gone?

First Love

In the summer of my sixteenth year I ached
with love for a honey blonde from Phillips
Mill. Knowing nothing of how hands move
over a girl's skin, I only sat on the grass
as she fed chicken legs to a burly end
from New Hope High. Later, when he buzzed
down the road in search of beer, she touched
her lips to mine and placed her hand
on the inside of my thigh. My hands hovered
like whirlybirds above her back. My face played setting
sun to the coming night.

She laughed, told me I was cute, and drove
me home, spinning her tires in my gravel
drive. I tripped, backwards, up my kitchen
steps, spun like Nureyev to bed, and dreamed
the way boys dream.

Morning came, I worked in my neighbor's yard,
chopping vines and carrying them away.
For weeks, my fingers touched—nothing.

Once, white-gloved, I passed her on the street,
holding up my hand to give a sign. She walked on
blankly—like Ophelia trailing daisies down
the stone stairs to the river. Her face was
bruised.

I have not seen her since, but sometimes
in summer when the itch comes I dream of her
the way boys dream.

Fool's Paradise

In my town it is dark by eleven.
Blue Fords sleep in grey garages
and the leaves are piled on curbs
in neat green bags. Muggers and
rapists pine from lack of work.
Even the dogs are silent, curled
in flealess dreams on thick shag rugs.

I dream of something different
like Halloween costumes at Sunday
tea, pumpkins on church steeples
and sheep painted Richard Petty blue
quietly eating the village green.

My parents never saw the sunrise sober.
They danced in fountains, trailing
the idols of the age from bar to bar
'til the liquor turned their minds
and my mother's fingers stiffened
on the keys and the notes echoed
sourly in the yellow dawn of Welfare
Island where they took her stomach out
and left her to die screaming
in the crowded halls. The hospital's
just a memory now, an item mentioned
on the Circle Line tour by guides
who say the price of condominiums
is high owing to the view.

In my town the people rise early
and the sun screams off the sugar
maples in the early fall. My sisters,

loosed from the dark arms of the cities
where they live, call it paradise.
I only tuck my tail under my doctor's
gown and grin. "For fools," I say.

Blood Talk

This one wades in thick hip boots,
grey green slick in the deep water,
purple fly pinned to the pocket
of the red flannel shirt. Flip of
the wrist and the line spins outward

...another spins yarns, crouched
on his wet thighs in the red shadow
of a Tennessee barn, spitting tobacco,
easy in the twilight air. Horses,
cows, pigs rut in the background.

And me? With no fisherman father,
no thicklipped mountain grandad,
no maiden aunt, starving, lace collared,
in the root cellar of her ante-bellum
home, no spittle drooling, Bourbon

drinking, twang talking uncles,
no chickens scratching in the yard,
no fast sweating mares, no garden,
my God, not even tomatoes or radishes,
or crosscut saw to cut winter wood.

I got nothing but goddam words working
for me, and everyone knows that words
aren't real, aren't flesh and blood,
and country-Southern like Bibles
and Red Man, and dreams, and blood.

Not Wisely But Too Well

The walls of my study are white, the door
and the shelves white. When the blinds
are pulled, even the windows are white.

If I sit a long time without speaking
I begin to believe that God will walk
in the door like cream rising to the top.

The other day I went to see my son
play soccer. He's tall with a summer
tan and sad soft eyes the girls like.

My heart pounds crazily for him. Up
and down the field he runs, then—crack!
He falls, Hector below the walls of Troy.

I swallow my heart and pray. Across the way
I see the other team—laughing. "You dirty
bastards!" I scream. My eyes blur. I run

toward them. "You're sick," I hiss into
their coach's ear. Blue shirted Trojans
circle my fallen son. I cannot look.

I sit in my white study and gaze
at the white walls. I wait for God
to enter. I watch...for signs.

Evening Light

The trees undress slowly from the top.
Bare arms arc brownly into the sky. It is
sunset. Orange skirts swirl in an awful
dying light. The ground is littered gold.

I stop the scene with the shutter of my eye—
stop and hold and mark—this blue, these reds
and holding greens—those rusts upon the ground.
I stoop and pick and hold this one dry leaf.

It crumbles in my hand, and I see a picture
from the morning paper speak as if alive.
Five Turkish children killed by earthquake
lie upon the ground, seemingly asleep.

The mother screams above, mouth horror ravaged,
while in Kentucky and Ohio other mothers weep
into clean white handkerchiefs as Taps is played
and flags are placed into their hollow laps.

Hats do not suffice. The time is never right.
Beauty is always almost gone. This dress, this
cock of the head, this touch, this curl of hair,
this greying beard, that look over the shoulder.

We are taken so suddenly, the breath goes
in white astonishment. If I had known is not
enough. Say it now. Say it now. Say it now.
Before the shutter clicks once more and closes.

Incarnation

Forget the virgin birth, the stable,
the cattle lowing and all that.
Maybe Mark was right...he just
arrives. John, waist-deep in water,
sees him first, striding toward Jordan,
hands bleeding, heels blistered
from walking barefoot down
the muddy ruts of roads.

He had never seen pain before. Never
watched a man die. In a thicket
one day he saw a fawn chew
its leg off to escape a trap.
Later he passed a corpse hanging
from a cross along the road.
So this is what it's like,
he thought. They'd never taught him
about pain up there.

So, he thinks, washing the dust off
in the river, feeling the touch
of John's hand upon his head,
this is what it means to be human.

Mary's Dream

"Did she put on his knowledge with his power...?"
—William Butler Yeats

Jesus at the lathe in the afternoon sun,
hairs blanding on the brown arms, nick
on the finger from some mishap
                       she at the window
frames the moment before the crazy
honeycombed John with his damned prophecy
comes upsetting Herod, starting heads rolling
and the sneer of the scribes unravelling
her son's life.
                     Who was Joseph anyway
to get her in this mess with his stupid
lineage?
                  And did she not dream, scream
nightly the hours on the cross, nails
in her own palms, waking at dawn, looking
across at his sleeping face and for an instant
so scared her breath stopped
                 being mother first
and God second   her son dying   why not someone
else's   what had she done anyway
                   blunt edged Joseph
would never understand the lake of glass
where they would stop and be left alone.

The New Magi

It is dusk. The sun has tipped backward
behind the old town hall. Inside the patterned
windows of the church, candles nod to candles
until it seems the world is only light
and festive voices singing "Silent Night."

Out of the dark the siren wails, once,
twice, a third time, and grinding gears
disturb the "all is bright," while somewhere
in another town a black man in a stocking cap
folds quilts around himself to stop the night.

Out of the dark the siren wails and somewhere
in another town a woman flushes yesterday's news
from under the rest room door and a red-haired girl
with shrouded eyes holds out her hand
to strangers walking through the station's

swinging doors. Where is the star that calls you,
black man? Where is the star that seeks you,
woman? Where is the star that lifts you, shrouded
girl? Walk to us, now, over the battered highways.
Walk to us slowly over the rutted roads.

Walk to the siren's wail, and the grunting sound
of fire in the night. Throw open the church's door.
Walk with your papers and your quilts and the sorrow
in your eyes, bringing your gifts past the carpet
of our candles to the manger's straw. Kneel and turn

And bid us follow with our light up the long aisle
out, out into the grace of the beckoning night.

Leavings
(for my father)

Outside my window a gnarled old oak
leans precariously on his elbow
snarling at his successors
wrapped smugly in their canvas diapers
and waiting
                    to be lowered
into the hard winter earth.

The other arm is gone,
the socket painted closed
with that preservative we use
to keep the old from rotting.

Knots bulge from his side like tumors.
Still
            I think I like him better
than all those thin skinned babies
packed tightly
                    in their little holes.

He's not so predictable.
In the spring he'll flower strangely
and dance his own configurations
in the wind.

Bless you, old brother.
May my leavings be so rich.

Good Friday

My son lounges before the television
his legs draped over the falling arm
of the chair, his eyes fixed on other
eyes, his lips tight. The story on

the screen is familiar. Jesus before
Pilate, but my son has never seen it—
not this way at least. Christ is sinewy,
lean, steel blue eyes piercing the flesh

of the soft politician. Pilate is easy.
He loves his wife, his wine, his silk sheets.
The fierce Sadduccees sicken him. He likes
Jesus, and I am drawn against my will

by the sudden nearness of the old tale.
My son and I are silent. We listen to the once
familiar words. Suddenly, voices in the hall
and lights from every side. Bags crinkle,

heels click on the wooden floor. My wife
is home from shopping, and with her a friend.
Skirted and hosed, armed in swatches,
they burst into the dark room where Pilate

stands, watching Jesus lashed and crowned.
They lay swatches of plums and cherries
on the couch's back. Jesus' back runs
with blood. They turn, open the French doors

to the next room, and laugh. The cherries
will not do for the curtains. They look toward
the ceiling. My son looks at the cross.
It is heavy. He watches Christ stumble, fall.

I hear the tinkle of cups and voices. My wife
is happy. Christ dies slowly. The blood seeps
from his palms and his shoulders twist like
splayed ropes. The Roman soldier laughs,

hands him vinegar to drink. My wife drinks
coffee with her friend. No, she says, the cherries
are too bright. Christ lies wrapped in white.
His mother kisses him. My wife's friend rises

and kisses her. She is pleased that they have
shopped so well. The rock is rolled before
the tomb. My son lounges, legs draped, in silence.

Out of Mourning

Spring again,
and I sit in the green chair reading.
The yellow dog noses among the neighbor's
daffodils. Over my book I watch for you
to come, waiting as I have all the nights
of my days for that moment beyond time
when April sorrows will be stilled by
the white flower in the moist red earth.

Did you know, my deep eyed dove, did you
know even then that August afternoon
as you danced in the willow's shade
that I who had been gone was standing
by the corner of the house watching
your whispered dreams?
                         Did you know
as you turned and looked and flowed
into my arms, locking your legs around
my waist, that you had hooked the very
marrow of my soul?
                       And did you know
that Easter morning as you cradled
the neighbor's child in your arms,
leaning your head against my knees
while I read in the April sun, that
the wind would blow over your grave
before another dawn?
                         Were these your gifts?
Waking or sleeping, I keep these images
inviolate, like mottled sunbeams through
winter windows or leaves long buried
in the beds of streams, kicked to the
surface by spring storms.

You grow
through the years. You are older
and the color in your cheeks runs
to red. Stand by my chair and put
your arms around my neck. Good.
I would feel that touch before another night.

Before Forty

"Why does it take men so long to grow up?"
—anonymous feminist

I'll tell you why. My mother drank a lot.
One night she shot my father. They separated.
Tough it out, little man, with no parents.
Tears are for girls, said the cops with the
silver badges and the yellow stripes on the
blue sleeves. Then the phone ringing,
I don't know, maybe five years later,
and me, twelve, in the bed, curled tight,
and my nightgowned sister at the door.
Christ, I know what it is before she even
opens it. I ought to cry, I think, because
my mother's dead, but dead eyes don't make
tears, do they?
                                    So we walk to the funeral
parlor in blue suits and dresses and me
dragged, silent, to look at a stranger
puffed up with rouge and lipstick and whatever
else they pour in the veins after the soul
flies. Then she was gone, and the sister
too, not dead, but swept, like Henry Fonda
and family in the *Grapes of Wrath*, kids in the
back seat reading Captain Marvel, boxes
tied with clothesline, husband at the wheel,
hair slicked down with Wildroot Cream Oil,
disappearing down the road to California.
Sweet Jesus, where was California, to a kid
nineteen years old who had to buy his own
bus ticket and didn't know how three thousand
miles could hurt. Tough it out, kid. You're
strong. Be a man.

Then, the daughter,
at thirty, as if the mother and the sister
weren't enough. To test him, maybe. Job.
Sitting in the church singing "O God Our
Help in Ages Past" and still dry eyed with
the rage helpless and blank and the room
upstairs suddenly empty and me walking the
steps in my sleep and coming home like Orpheus
empty handed.
                    Come on, now, ladies, you do
like that? Then the crack up, the spinning
edgeward of the top on the kitchen table and
the Humpty Dumpty business of trying to make
a jewel of the cracked pieces of the heart.

So you want a happy ending? I don't know
much about that. I cry a lot these days.
Not for broken shoelaces or spilled beer,
but for Bach and the Beatles and for
beauty where I find it. I sleep later,
dream more, and write stuff like this.

After

After the grass has been trimmed and
the beans picked, the flowers watered,
creeping plants plucked, and the dog
checked for fleas and ticks and other
crawling insects and the ants swept
from the kitchen floor into neat green
bags for disposal in the proper place

After the children have been marched
to the store for their fall clothing
and the drawers rearranged and the ten
year old cries in his brother's shirt
and the oldest flies to college, and the
youngest's behavior has been modified
by Montessori and the spouse sent packing
to the latest conference on conferences

After the course on small engine
repairs has been completed and the
automobiles, power motors, racing boats,
refrigerators, washing machines, dryers,
fans, and hair blowers have each been
meticulously disassembled, diagnosed
and surgically mended

4

After the United States Government has been
consulted and the pamphlets rigorously read
with special attention to italics and the
changes in tax law memorized and all the
proper forms duly filled out and notorized

5

After the Sunday Times has been read
in bed and crossword and jigsaw puzzles
pieced together and the Orange, Rose, Sugar,
Wintergreen, Spearmint, Tangerine, Wool, and
Lucite Bowls argued over, slept through,
and Saturday Night Live jived, and Archie
Bunker booed for the ninety-ninth time, and
Playboy plucked from the fourteen-year-old

6

After the face is made up, the collar tightened,
the tie tied, the girdle stretched, the dress
bought, the shoes shined, the stockings seamed,
the red coat returned for the beige, and
the luggage bought for the trip to France
and the smiles smiled, and the passports
paid for, and the Florida sun burns the
arms pink instead of brown

7

After the cousins are kissed and the grandparents
thanked and the old friends courted anew and
the tennis rackets resurrected once more for

the mayor's annual game and the tuxedo and
evening gown rented for the club ball and
the gold pen received for thirty years of
faithful service, and the hair rinsed to
take away the grey, and the teeth capped

8

After the sun has set, and the moon, and the
stars, and candles, and lanterns, and electric
lights, and fireflies, and the windows nailed
shut and the doors locked and the VACANT
sign placed in the yard, and the dogs lift their
legs in the long grass

9

Then I will...then you will...then we

FROM
A SMALL THING LIKE A BREATH

1993

A Small Thing Like A Breath

For James and Robert

How cheap words are. How easy to say,
"I love you," knowing not even the surface
of the word. How easy to say, "I'd die for you,"
knowing not even the icy edge of death, not even
his outer garments.

Then you bear a child. You carry a life
in the darkness of your womb for nine uneasy
months. The child descends, bumping the fragile
edges of its unformed skull against the walls
of your pelvic bone. He enters the world wailing.

For a time the machines help him breathe.
You cannot hold him because of the wires,
the sensors which monitor each vital function
and so you sit by his side and give him your
finger to hold, and you watch his tiny,
perfectly formed nails curl around you
and after many hours you are still not tired,
not finished marveling at the wonder you have
created and you know that you could, indeed
would die for this son, this glorious, heartbreaking,
selfish, beautiful son.

              And every night you continue
to marvel, week after week, month after month.
Every night before sleep you tiptoe into his room
and listen to each small breath and watch the way
he seems to smile and how his eyelashes curl upward.
And later you will keep pictures, you will mark
his first step and the awkward, rounded shapes
of his first letters. You will shout with joy

for his first line drive and cry for the pink
cotton sheep he makes in Sunday school on Easter.

And when he hurts you will know the very marrow
of love, how pain for his pain takes you
in its arms and grips like icy night. Then,
when you speak of love and death, you will do so
not lightly, but with bowed head and hushed respect
for a small thing like a breath.

Growing Up

Why do they call it *up*? Why not growing *out*?
or older or colder, but certainly not bolder.
If *up* is the long mouthed faces who drive
their barred cars to work down the choking asphalt
roads, then I'm for *down* or even *back*.

You know the grown up guy in the ad who's eating
frosted flakes with Tony the Tiger chuckling
over his shoulder? Well, that's me. Why not?

What's so hot about up? Where's the Lorax
in up? Where's Jiminy Cricket wishing on a star
in the forest where the wild things are?

My world is a tea-party. No, not a lip pursing
finger-lifting, tight-assed tea party. A real one.
The maddest of Mad-Hatter tea parties, and everyone's
invited. There's Curious George swinging
from the branches with Dumbo and Eeyore
and Horton, and little Cindy Lou Who cheering
them on. There's Homer Price and Tom Sawyer
and Christopher Robin making donuts like demons
and swapping tall tales with Sam I Am
and Miss Muffet and the Spider sitting down
beside each other and Snow White and Cinderella
and Sleeping Beauty comparing hair—and princes
and Tom and Jerry and Sylvester and Tweetie Bird
and even Wiley Coyote and the Road Runner laughing
so hard at their own cartoons that tears are coming
from their eyes and Hansel and Gretel and Dorothy
and the Scarecrow cheering for the death of wicked
witches and Roo and Kanga and Piglet shouting

hooray for the little engine that could
and Peter making Captain Hook walk the plank
while Tinker Bell shines from up on high and
all the fairy godmothers descend to give
their blessings at the end.

How does that sound? How does that compare with *up*?
So the next time someone yells at you, "Grow Up,"
just say—no thanks—I'm going for *down* or *in*
or *back*. Anything but *up*.

My Dog, The Lover

seventy-five at least in human years
has fallen for a tawny, spaniel bitch
six houses down the street but uphill
all the way. He sits with other suitors

in the cool of her garage. He spurns
me as I drive by. I stop, clap my hands,
entreat him home with slurping sounds
of supper and hints of tummy rubs.

He stretches lazily, cocking an eye
at the black lab next to him as if to say
those humans are such bores. He rises,
lifts a leg to wet a dandelion, ambles

to the car and sits, head held high,
in the front passenger seat. At home
I let him out and turn my head to fetch
the groceries from the rear. Before I turn

again, he's gone, flashing up the hill,
this white haired Romeo on pads, tail out,
feathers fluffed. To hell with him, I say,
let him starve, let him feed on love.

Ten minutes pass. Thunder rumbles in the west.
I laugh and wait the count of five. Sure enough,
like Mercury pursued by Mars, he races to my
side, this Don Juan of dogdom, hiding his head
between my legs and trembling like a child.

Far From Home

But suppose you've *been* home and know
the very taste of home, not the bacon
frying taste, but soul taste, tongue
taste, and the touch, the very fingers
of home, the voice, cry in the heart,
clutch in the throat of home. Not
the pictures on the wall and mama's
apron strings, but the tooth smile
and the spirit swept into the last
row of peace and the head-shaking,
arm-swinging, foot-stomping, bone-rattling
shit-shaking taste of home.

                I mean, suppose
you've known that, seen it, smelt it,
touched the very perfume of it, had it
in the billows of your gills, friend?

And then you got kicked out into the ice,
into the flat black frying pan of every day
and squatted in the grey brown grass
of what they call life and then some dude
who thought he knew something tried to save
you, tried to tell you what home was and how
to get there and you *knew* because you've
been, friend,—I mean, then, it gets tough
because what you had you remember like live
roses in winter, like fresh fish in an arctic

freeze. Like you know it, but you can't get
at it, and nobody cares because they don't
believe you know anything anyway.

Don't talk home to me,
friend. I've been there. And after that,
well after that, the world's just somewhere
to walk through. It looks pretty, it looks
like something—but under the red leaves
and the holly berries, you're still waiting
for home to come back and catch you in her
arms, as if she knew, as if she still cared.

Christmas Vespers

Grandfathers straining to hear, baby
sisters in starched petticoats, brothers
in unfamiliar ties, alien cars packed
along the leaf-strewn streets, they come
for the annual miracle as if the voices,
as if the bright-tongued girls and
ruby-throated boys could lift them,
touch them to eternity in this one
forgetting hour.

No room in the inn,
I perch like a great horned owl
in the balcony below the organ loft,
hooting curses on all this holiness.
My gut aches tonight, and I cannot
listen for the pain.

Once I too could make
tunes and see the smile of God in the
flickering candle's light. I too could
redraw time's face in the caverns
of my mind. I too could sing to asking
eyes of strangers and of friends.

Now, from my uneasy perch, I think
of shouting "Fire!" to watch them
tumble toward the doors in sudden fear.

Somewhere in the dark out there
the stable waits.

Of Catchers
For Andy

in the rye and elsewhere I can only say
it is a matter of timing. These kids,
you know, running through the deep field,
not seeing the cliff and you there, noble you,
with your big hands grabbing one. Great.
But the next one tumbles screeching down below
into the whatever. The field is too damned
big, the kids are everywhere. You see?

Or the girl, the trapeze artist, swinging
her long legs out-once, twice, she flips
then grasping the rod behind her knees
back and forth, back and forth, she rocks
and launches out into the sweet nest
of your waiting hands.

                    But you, you're
swinging back, reaching now for air itself,
watching her fingers one last time stretching
for you as she falls.

                    Catching. It's bruised thumbs
and busted bones in every joint and a cold
smack in the soul every time you lose one.

So drop it, son, so to speak. Now.

The Poet, The Lovers, And The Nuns

I.

It is cool for June. The sky, shockingly blue,
aggravates the poet's dreams. He curses
the littered streets and the soft fingered
hustlers of the alleys. Shaking the rust
of solitude, he mounts the hill to the Cloisters.

The lovers are already there, twining their fingers
like the necks of swans on the gray stones of the parapets.
Their eyes shine with joy. The poet passes by.

Below, five sisters all in white emerge
from the Madison Avenue bus. In his mind's
eye the poet sees them, ducks in a row, their thin black-
stockinged ankles crossed in unison,
riding the tarred streets, mouths wide
at the blinding sights of the city's carnival.
Now they are safe, now they have come home.

II.

In Robert Campin's room the lovers laugh.
Their legs touch easily like old friends.
He whispers, she smiles and looks at Campin's
little man sliding on beams of light straight
toward the Virgin's ear. Out back, Joseph
makes mousetraps to catch the devil, while
the poet watches from the curving stairs.

III.

The sisters have found the room of the unicorn
tapestries. They are aroused. They chatter
gravely in muted whispers like children
after dark. The poet is angry. He cannot hear.

They are young. They carry their love for Christ
in the pockets of their hearts. They are white
with hope. Piece by piece they follow the hunt.
They taste the drool of hate in the hunters' mouths.
Bite and stab, bite and stab, bite and stab.
They cry silently within. It is their Lord,
their dearest God who bleeds for them.

All at once the smallest gives a startled
cry. She sees the flowered resurrection.
Her sisters gather near in watchful silence,
worshipping without words. The poet lurks
under the hunters watching.

IV.

The lovers have found "The Unicorn in Captivity."
They did not know that anything so beautiful
existed. Their hearts are the colors of flowers.
They see the face of God in each other's eyes.
Millefleurs say the French. A thousand flowers,
and somewhere there the lovers are lost. They are
past saving.

The poet thinks of politics. What use is art
if you're starving? After the revolution peasants
stormed the palaces and for fifty years the tapestries
warmed the tops of turnips and radishes,
beets and green beans. The poet likes the irony.

V.

The sisters are tired. They sit on the wooden bench
facing the fragrant garden. They breathe the scent
of summer herbs. All in white, they watch the sky.

The lovers rest opposite them against the stone.
He cradles her in his arms, covers her eyes. They are
suspended in the slant whispers of nodding leaves.

The poet is sick. He has seen too much.
He misses the sound of horns in the checkered
streets. He boards the A train, downtown side,
Graffitied posters are manna to his eyes.

The Beginning

You see, I have forgotten everything
except the loving. I do not know
about the kissing, the placement
of the hands or the lips or whether
the tongue goes this way or that.

I do not know any more about the touching
or the movement of limbs
or the freedom of the eyes to watch
or whether anything is wanted
or how one knows desire. I remember

only that on certain nights
when the full moon hung low on the horizon
there was the beginning
of something more than you and me
something more than self

and if I lost that forever
it would be losing God
or whatever God is. To save that
I would perform a hundred tasks
pluck a thousand blossoms,

do penance under some saint's rock
if only it would lead
to a blue door in the green wood.
I would unlive it all
so we could again begin.

Ely Cathedral: Toward Evensong

Not dusk but its semblance, rain making
the stones cold, March damp, gray sky
blanketing both towers, only the greenness
of grass hinting at July. We shuffle through
western doors, umbrellas dripping. Another
day, another page in the Baedeker.
My wife drifts to the tearoom to warm
her hands. She will read her romance.

I walk down the painted nave expecting little.
Too many days, too many aisles, too many Norman
arches. I remember the words of my professors.
Clerestory, I murmur, and triforium. My head
knows the beauty of these forms, but heart
has flown to landscapes of home. I kneel
in a front pew and close my eyes. I speak
the names of absent friends. I call up faces.

From somewhere music. Beyond me, in the choir,
boys rehearse for evensong. "Kyrie," they sing,
"Kyrie eleison." "Christ have mercy," I echo,
"have mercy," and all at once I see—not boys—
but wheelchairs circling the altar before me,
wheelchairs with children of all ages, who cannot
speak or move their limbs. Muscleless, they sprawl,
heads propped by braces, eyes crossed absently.

I am frightened. My heart beats wildly. In the
choir the boys sing again, their voices pure
as night before first light, while one by one
attendant women turn the children's heads upward.

They point to the light above and all at once
mind and eyes remember the octagon of Ely
and those giant beams of oak hoisted to hold
the glass of the lantern and the eight-pointed
golden star which binds the dome. The children
hear the music, see the cunning of the craft,
the many fingered dome, they sense as I cannot,
the painted hand of God. My eyes swim, knees
ache from the dense wood. I look again into
the lantern's light and down into the children's
eyes. What do they think? Do they ask why God
creates such wondrous sights and helps them

not at all? Do they scream within? I butt
my head against the kneeling rail and watch
their eyes again and the soft hands of the nurses.
Ask them, says my better self, but my lips
spell only silence, legs stalk awkwardly away.
In the bookstore I will read of Etheldraeda,
saint of Ely Isle, who married twice
and still remained intact. That will be good.

Dust Beneath My Shoe

Her marker rests beyond the centerfield fence
under a mulberry tree. The boys once, chasing
a long home run, found the ball nestled near
her name. I had not told them where she was,
for they had come later and we had shrouded
the sad past, buried her beyond the lawns
of their green memories. They knew of her,
of course, and stared with inward eyes, tracing
the shapes of the letters with their fingers.

The dirt of place marks the patterns of our lives.
"Where you from?" the natives ask with the slow
drawl and easy sense of ownership only time
in Southern towns can bring. "From here," I say.
They smile, knowing the accent is foreign,
and ask again, slyly, "Where'd you *come* from?"

"New York," I say, when my daughter rests blessedly
only a boy's throw past the centerfield fence,
and thirty miles down the old highway to Charlotte
in the city cemetery, mother and grandmother lie
in unmarked graves. New York is good enough,
where mother, lonely for grandmother's ghost, died in '51
and shuttled down the narrow hall of memory into—
for all I knew and cared—nothingness, until one day,
like the boys, quite by accident, I found her name
in the register—Frances Hayden Covington—Faith,
Hope and Charity, she used to say—of the old public
cemetery down the road.

"Where you from?" they ask again, knowing no Charleston
cousins or Spartanburg aunts, knowing the car stays

in the gravelled drive on holidays. "From here," I say
to the dust beneath my shoe. And still they ask,
"But where'd you *come* from?"

Remembrance

The spring rises from the earth, root to stem
blossom to leaf. Each day catches the breath
like a song remembered, forgotten then found
again. In a night the Bradford pears turn
white to green and tulips splash in haunting
reds by my neighbor's door.

You rise like the season. Your face shines
in the pools along the road as I walk
to the grave yard. I pass the old house.
You glide down the stairs and take my hand.
We share the season. Is it hyacinth or lilac
I smell? I lie in the grass beside your stone.
I watch the bees work in the crossed branches
of the blooming apple tree. The sky shines beyond.

I bring you my anger and my pain. I hand
them to you like bread. I speak the loaves
of my sorrow, the broken pieces of my rage.
I have beaten the trees in my back yard wood
till my hands turned blue from gripping
the pounding stick. I have known knuckle
blood and screams in the soundless throat.

Now I hug the earth, pressing my chest to the growing
grass, spreading my arms outward. I close my eyes
and wait. The anger drains like water after rain.

You smile at my smallness, you kiss my folly
with your parted lips. "Sit," you say,
and I squat with you cross-legged like some
novice guru. "Kneel," you say, and the stone
cuts the letters of your name into the memory
of my knees. "Eat," you say, and my mouth opens
like the yawning bird's. "Taste," you say,
and your sugared love charms the buds of my tongue.

I rise like one groggy after dreaming. I stagger
homeward on the cracked sidewalk into the back yard
of the old house. Everywhere, in the knee-high grass
spring flowers bloom madly.

Stirring The Muse
for Stephen

1.

She will be courted, wooed. As fickle as the sun
in an English spring. I take her to France.
Chenonceau, I say, in my sweetest manner.
The name rolls off my lips like time itself,

but still she will not bend. I march her down
the long gallery, play her Vivaldi, place my arm
around her waist and lead her to the window where
the water runs in black streams under white arches.

Open-mouthed, I take the rain in my face, I place
my hands upon her cheeks and kiss her, once,
twice, three times upon the lips, and still she will not
speak. Her eyes look past me to the tree behind.

I turn, and she is gone. I limp, goat-footed
to the waiting car and murmur curses in my wet coat.

2.

For you, it's easy, knowing as you do the quick
rush of beauty into the flat, black night. Knowing
as you do how mountains thrust like newly sighted
eyes out of the landscape's sullen face. For you

she comes like a fine turn of mind cycling
the twisting hills, burning the brain like sand
in Sardinia, like grey stone in Budapest, like
Paris in April rain, cobblestones stained

with wine, bridges over the Seine, whispers
at night as the train winds whitely into Swiss
hills. She feeds you from her mouth, sings
into your soul. Your heart warms darkly to her song.

3.

I wait, like an old bear after winter sleep.
I prowl the halls, scratching my back on the closed
doors. Inside, voices drone like my grandfather's
Evinrude. Students drool on their notes, pencils

clatter to the floor, elbows slipping sidewise
heads bouncing off the rude desks. You laugh. Good.
I move from room to room. Invisible, I peek.
Nothing here but shoes and the shapes of old notes.

Nothing here but sad backward moments
of texts untaught. You know. Good. Mark it with blood.
You'll make a teacher. She'll have you all right.
She loves the daring, the hungry, and the young,

askers of hard questions, senders of messages
in bottles, sleepers under the open air. And me?
I still scratch and growl under the leaves,
searching for that further spring.

Words Are The Only Fingers Of The Soul

1.

I wake at five in the morning
　　　full moon shining on the lake
　　　　　and think of you swimming

in your own thick waters
　　　buoyed up by that absurd faith
　　　　　I have never had that whatever

lurked, slippery, in the green deep
　　　wished you no harm.
　　　　　This has always been your hour,

too bright for night, too still for dawn
　　　when nothing is either right or wrong
　　　　　but simply, beautifully, *is*.

I try to place you. I grope
　　　through the atlas, state by state,
　　　　　searching the name of your town

the numbers of highways
　　　as if names and numbers like talismans
　　　　　could roll the rock from your door.

Words are the only fingers of the soul
　　　words spoken and heard
　　　　　written and received

like hands thrust deep into bowls
　　　of ripe cherries, then pulled,
　　　　　　burgundy stained, into the air.

2.

I see you now as a child of nine
        riding the thin mountain road
                in your father's Ford,

hill steep, tight with laurel on one side,
        the other a bank falling down,
                down and suddenly three wild ponies

bolt before your eyes—roan, dapple, black—
        I don't know, I must invent,
                and the father, angry, pushing

obscenely down on the reluctant pedal,
        ponies, eyes in panic rolling
                like your own, and your words

"Please, Daddy, please," the car closing
        the manes waving, sweat on their haunches
                small feet kicking dust

and the ponies sliding, tumbling over the side
        in your mind's eye
                or smashing blood-full

into the Ford's grill, the father laughing,
        maybe, as you scream
                and cover your eyes

fingernails cutting the skin
        above your blond brows
                drawing blood.

Then, an opening, unforeseen,
        the ponies veer, vanish
                into the thick dark green

and the father unrelenting still
        points the snarling car
                downward to hellmouth.

3.

We thirst for news
        we die for want of story.
                Tell me more, the heart cries.

I know now when you make the horse noise
        in the throat you are one
                with your wild sisters

open mouthed in their flawless pain.
        We are one with the animals, you say.
                I know, I understand. I see

you dancing, breasts free, feet bare
        skirt swirling, hair fresh
                washed from the summer lake

in that wilder wood of your imagining
        neighing under the maddening moon
                while my fingers write these words.

Carrot Colored Words
For Kappa and Jay

The dialogue goes something like this:
"I love you," I say, it being the end
of our conversation. "I love you,"
you sigh weakly after long silence.

I challenge your desultory reply.
"It's the word," you say. "It's been
overused. We need to find a better."
I accept the task. For nights I search

for carrot colored words, for words
with tails and purple horns and long
red sashes round their middles. I scream
for green words with yellow spotted stomachs.

My doctor friend tells me how patients
miss medical terms. A woman in Georgia
spoke of suffering from "Smiling Mighty
Jesus," meaning spinal meningitis.

Another had "Fireballs of the Eucharist,"
in reality fibroids of the uterus. If I
could choose, I'd take Jesus too. And those
fireballs beat fibroids all to hell.

That's the kind of word I want. I fireball
you. I smiling mighty Jesus you. It's cute
and satisfies your need for something new
but it's not exactly what I mean to say.

What I mean to say is—if I were dying
and I could choose one person in the world
to sit and hold my hand and hear whatever
words I had to say—it would be you

and I know no better term for that
than love. If I find one, I'll let you know.

FROM
THE SEARCH FOR WONDER
IN THE CRADLE OF THE WORLD

2000

Genesis
For Stephen and Katy

The swinging Lord, that master maker
of cool chords, shifted in his empty
heaven and said, "I need me some music."

So the sky was full of music
and he declared that it was good.

And then the equally androgynous Lord
said to herself, I need some light
to fill the fragrant fingers of the night.

So the waters shone with light
and she declared that it was good.

And when the light and the music played
together the stars wept for the beauty of it.
And the swinging, singing Lord said

I need me some people to praise
this thing that I have made.

The Lord thought long and long about what
sort of people might be the purest praisers,
what sort of people might truly see the light.

And he made man, with his cunning brain,
and he made the zebras and the elk
and the swift running antelope for man

to wonder at. And she made woman with her
imagining mind and her long, limber dancing
legs and her eyes that saw the color in the light

And when the man and woman had been crafted
The Lord declared that it was good.
Then the man heard the light in the woman's eyes
And the woman saw the music in the man's mind
And the music was the silky manes of violins

And the light was like the laughter of clarinets
and the glitter of guitars. And the man and the
woman moved to the measure of the music and swayed

to the gold and amber brilliance of the light.
And they knew that the sound was neither his nor hers
nor like anything that ever was before.

And the Lord saw what they had made
And behold it was very good.

Alphabet Soup

Soon the words will mix like the jumbled
letters in alphabet soup sliding down
the throat finally to mingle in the stomach
with other things. Will it hurt, this loss?

Will I know, when it happens, that it is
happening? Today I tried to find the name
of someone, a man who coaches at my school.
He played basketball with Michael Jordan.

He is tall with slightly graying hair
and he bears the same name as some other
player, an even taller man. The one I know
is white, the other one is black.

At the game on Tuesday night a girl came up
and hugged me. I hugged her back. I asked her
how she was, and she presented me with her
beautiful four-year-old daughter. She took

classes with me, and acted in many plays.
Her name has slipped away.
It is like that now. Cells destructing
by the millions. Synapses sputtering.

Words like the jumbled letters of alphabet
soup, tumbling, tumbling down.

The Photograph: Fifty Years After
For Nancy

The boy had only wanted to see her in white,
and walk her down the aisle, there being
no father to give her away. After all, she
was his sister, and she had promised.

For years he lamented her betrayal, her eloping
with the slick piano player from Georgia,
Sea Island honeymoon and all, while he was marooned
in that yellow boarding school between cold sheets.

Now he knows better. Now, fifty years later
he knows better. He has seen the photograph,
where she sits, hair parted in the middle,
gardenias pinned above the ear, white blouse,
blue jacket, head cast down—slight hint
of shyness—eyes looking up with hope,
and a smile as young as creation's first day.

All that hope, that radiance. There she sits,
high school graduate, life before her, smiling
at the world. And why? What had she to smile
about? Youth, beauty, and a mother so drunk
they'd shipped her off to the state funny farm—
no Betty Ford clinics in those days. Stepfather
gone, vanished into the hoodlum streets of New York,
and the girl alone in the house, eighteen,
no job, no money and the landlady crying
for the rent. This smile, and for whom?

For the landlady, who relented, took the girl
into her own home, rented the empty house—
for the landlady who just happened to be

a photographer and the girl was looking for
a job, no high school picture to submit,
nothing but the clothes on her back. So what
the heck, it was the least she could do

for this girl who would go to a bar one night
and fall for the sweet fingers of the piano
player. No wonder they bolted. And the boy,
away at camp and then at the yellow school
wondering where she was, not knowing about
the mother or the rent or how hard it was
just to be a girl of eighteen with nothing
but hope and a smile and the scent of white
gardenias in her hair.

One Talent Man

He also who had received the one talent came forward, saying, "Master I knew you to be a hard man, reaping where you did not sow and gathering where you did not winnow; so I was afraid, and I went and hid your talent in the ground. Here you have what is yours."

—Matthew 25: 24-25

As a kid I had it cold. Get five make five.
The school I went to had a Latin motto:
"Poteris Modo Velis"—You Can If You Will.
It was easy. Get three make three, and so on.

I read it in the Bible my mother gave me
for my ninth birthday. I underlined the words
in red. It was simple—except for the one
talent man. He was different. He was a slob.

He was fat—with pimples. Zits. A jerk,
a nerd, a nobody, a rotting heap of vegetation,
a stupid, useless fool. God was fair.
The kid was no good. He got what he deserved.

Now I don't know. Seriously, I don't know.
Maybe the servant got a raw deal. Maybe
he was lame or halt or blind. One talent
isn't much. Maybe he thought usury was

wrong. "You ought to have invested my money
with the bankers," the master says. Whoa!
In the Old Testament they kill people
for doing that. I see him out there at night

burying the beautiful talent in the earth,
watching the dirt slowly cover the burnished
gold. Maybe he'd shined it one last time
before he let it go. Well, it would be safe

at least, he thought. And then this master,
this God, casting him into outer darkness
and all that. And I think—this guy is me,
ME—not some pimpled slob down the block.

And the five and three talent men standing
by so smug, so satisfied, smirking at each
other like the guy in the popular song
they call sixty minute man. Thirty seconds,

is what I am. Then there's this weeping
and gnashing of teeth, and for what?
I mean, where's the grace, God, for the
poor slob who buried it in the ground?

What Do Men Want?

"Drums, sweat, and tears," says *Newsweek
Magazine*, telling of wild-man weekends
in the woods and tales of missing fathers
in the sweat-house. It's not so simple.

In my fifteenth year my mother died.
Embarrassed not to cry, I tucked my head
under the sheets and feigned tears
for my older sister's eyes and ears.

In my thirtieth year on the Monday
after Easter my daughter went to bed
and never woke. Strong men carried her out.
Her arm hung down below the stretcher's

side. Dry-eyed I picked it up and put
it back. At thirty-five I struck
a boy for stealing from my son.
I spun and spun, darkly off balance,

hearing my voice, as if a stranger's,
ringing in distant ears. By forty
I learned the stepping stones of grief
and how the smallest things are joined.

Bach and the Beatles and "Amazing Grace,"
the quaking aspen leaves and sugar maples
in the fall could set me off on cue.
At fifty I fake colds instead of tears,

blowing my nose at "Thelma and Louise."
What do men want? I don't know.
The right to grieve and not be mocked,
to touch and be touched, to walk

beyond the porch steps of the soul,
to have dreams and speak them without fear.
To lie under the willow tree of love.
To seek truth in whispers not in shouts.

I like that better than drumming.

Aids by Transfusion

In memory of Desha Rosborough

> *"…we turn him into an anecdote to dine out on. Or dine in on.*
> *But it was an experience. I will not turn him into an*
> *anecdote. How do we fit what happened to us into life*
> *without turning it into an anecdote with no teeth and a*
> *punch line you'll mouth over and over for years to come."*
> —John Guare, *Six Degrees of Separation*

On the corner of Broadway and Sixty-Seventh Street
near the Opera with the flash of its Marc Chagall
murals, near the symphony, near the Vivian Beaumont
Theatre from whose plush red seats we had just risen

a man sits huddled in a blanket, silent, his message
printed in block letters on his cardboard box.
"Aids by transfusion," it reads. "Need 64 dollars
for bus ticket to Florida." My friend bends to him.

She whispers words I cannot hear. He whispers
back. She pulls three twenties from her purse
and stuffs them, crumpled, in his groping hand.
He smiles in thanks through wounded teeth.

In the play we had just seen, a black man cons
rich New Yorkers. He pretends to be the bastard
son of Sidney Poitier. He promises them parts
in the film of Cats. He takes their money and vanishes.

My friend feeds the homeless on Friday nights
driving by their cardboard boxes under bridges
with blankets and food and sweaters for the cold.
She calls them all by name. She loves them.

"Do you think it's true, his story about AIDS?"
I ask her as we cross the street. "Does it
matter?" she snaps, and walks ahead as if
I am not there. "Wait!" I call and follow after.

Treasure Hunt

For Karl Plank

> *"The kingdom of heaven is like treasure hidden in a field,*
> *which a man found and covered up; then in his joy*
> *he goes and sells all that he has and buys that field."*
> —Matthew 13:44

I have been thinking of this since Thursday,
the field with the treasure in it, and what
it looked like, trying to picture the guy
walking along the road beside an ordinary
field with wild flowers he doesn't even
know the name of—a guy like you or me.
He isn't out trying to find treasure,
but just walking and admiring the beauty
of the day, late September, the morning air
crisp like fresh lettuce, and he sees it
by mistake even, and he rubs his eyes
because—well, because—he's never seen
anything like this before, and his first
thought is he's either blind or crazy.
It's like, as you said, Karl, find the
hidden object in the picture. You look
and look and look and never see it, and then
one day—dum de dum—you're walking along
and boom! There it is. And you're in big
trouble, because now your whole life has
changed. Oh shit, you think. I can't do this.
I'm just an ordinary guy. I don't need
this. I know what happens to those people
that win the lottery. Who wants a million?
It's nothing but stress and taxes.

So he goes home, and carries on as if
he's just the same, but he isn't and he

never will be again. That's the joy, Karl,
and the pain, too. Because after that, the
things the world wants—the suits and cars
and even trout stuffed with crab meat—aren't
ever quite the same either. So he keeps sneaking
back to catch a glimpse of the treasure, which
he's covered up of course in case some other
guy should come along and spot it (which must
be a mistake since God says the treasure is for
everyone). And every time he gets a glimpse
his heart goes bonkers. It's so beautiful
it freaks him out. It makes him want to laugh
and cry and scream at the same time, like
Mozart's Requiem sung right. But he knows if
he takes it he'll have to give up everything.

And that's tough, because he's got a house
on the lake and a Honda Accord and he really
does still like the trout despite what I said,
and everything—EVERYTHING, DAMMIT, IS EVERYTHING.

Then one day he goes back, and the treasure—
well, I bet you didn't expect this—the treasure
is gone. His heart sinks—all the way down, below
the knees. "Shit happens." Sure it does, but you
can't blame this one on God. It was there, you
could have taken it, but you didn't. And now
he knows. It was the treasure made the house,
the car, the trout worthwhile. Without the treasure,
who cares? Without the treasure, where's the joy?
It's the treasure brings the joy. But we—we're
so dumb, we don't know that until it's gone.

The man in the parable, he was much smarter than
we are. He was onto something…very, very big.

The Missing Heron
For Sara Beasley

In the long grass on the other bank, the heron
stands. If he sees me, my presence does not
disturb him. He does not fly, but if I moved,
say, or threw a stone in the smooth water
he would take wing.

                        And so I speak to you
silently in my mind while I watch
the heron on the distant bank. You see, something
has happened. In my office, where the leaves glow
gold in the late October sun outside
my window, the students are strangely silent.
They speak only of their grades and the ways
they can gain credit for their work abroad.

I know how long they wait outside your door
to watch you listen with that light behind
your eyes, how you smooth the jagged edges
of their wounds and sing them into life.

I only want what I cannot have, something back
which is lost like that last thrust of the October
sun through the yellow leaves, like the heron
who stood near the other bank when I began
these thoughts. I never saw him fly away
though I was looking toward him as I spoke.

What We Have

1.

Back roads curving through fields of cotton,
rough balls left by the pickers, brown tilled
soil still soft in the afternoon sun, sugar
maples screaming orange and red, tobacco smell
in weathered barns, children walking, packs
slung easy over shoulders, men talking
by roadside pumpkin stands.
                                                Sun slipping,
sand smooth on now bare feet, waves breaking
suddenly violet on the empty beach, ocean
glimmering gold as we stand, astonished,
at the moment's gift.
                                    Later we speak, touching
easily like cousins, bantering, bourbon in hand,
on the creekside dock as the moon rises, mirrored
in the still water.

2.

Morning on the river, birds circling, their nests
topping the marker poles. We turn down smaller
streams, then glide through arches made by spreading
oaks. No engine now, only the whir of line
and plop of lure, crookback minnow, purple worm,
flipped with the quick wrist under the twining vines.

3.

Night and the waves beat deep into the rhythm
of our dreams. Salt-tossed, we wake then sleep
again. I wake early, take the beach alone.

Willets, pipers gather for church, sleep through
bird sermon, one-legged, heads tucked under wings.
A solitary girl stares at the spray from the jetty's
end. I walk northward and wait for the sea to speak.

4.

Lingering, champagne in the noon sun, toes
in sand, we watch the ocean give us one last show. We hug
good-bye then see the reeds turn golden
in the creek. We leave before the sun, over
the bridge and into the orange woods. We speak
little. Our hearts devour what we have seen
and heard and smelt, pictures to thaw the winter
dark, what we have instead of God, instead of love.

Sunset on Skiff Mountain

Sunset on Skiff Mountain, and the snow
silent and white as a bride's veil.
Wednesday afternoons in winter I drive
the winding road from the shadowed valley
and marvel at the moment the sun breaks
through the arms of the sleeveless trees,
marvel how in this hour before dark
light is restored like Joseph to his brothers
in Egypt after the long lean years. I stand
by the pond in the fallow fields in utter
gratitude. Something here is given,
some grace we never had to earn.

If I died tonight I would take this
with me, like the letter O. O, I would say,
And O and O and O again.

The sun lowering and the distant hills
like slumbering giants, beckoning—
beckoning.

Point of Light

For Susan and Kevin

We know so little. Who is to say what
truth is? When the door has been closed
and the light turned off for the night,
who is to say what goes on in that room

we call God? Who is to say what God
thinks or knows about our pain and why
we have it. In the case of a child
we think the worst. Yesterday I thought

of my daughter who died so many
years ago, and how I talked to God
then and said, "All right, you've done
the worst and I'm still here."

And how I burned with anger, helpless
with rage, and how later she came
to my son in a dream, beautiful
and whole and grown into woman

and told him she was well, told
him not to fear. And I think of you
now in your pain and how you must
ask God every day why Jack should

hurt so much and how it is only
later we can know anything at all.
So for now, think of your courage
as a gift, and think of each small

step down the hall, each nurse's
touch, each friend's voice as God.
Think Donna and Eileen and Pat
think of the cells themselves created

like the universe from nothing
and that strange emptiness under
the pain where God starts to work—
and how he shines there, glows

in the marrow of these new bones.

Walking on Water

On the waterside in Tiberias, the city
the Romans made, bearded peddlers hawk
golden "feesh, two for a dollar."

Pilgrims board boats for Capernaum,
billed as "the home town of Jesus"
in the slick magazines, a thirty-minute

ride north on a nice day, though
the Sea of Galilee, as we all know,
is prone to sudden storms, especially

in early spring. On the upper deck
the captain sells sea-shell bracelets
made by sailors' wives. Below, pilgrims

sing hymns they know by heart. When
the wind comes up, I'm standing
at the rail musing on how Jesus walked

across the lake and the disciples
scared in their small boat. We huddle
below with the pilgrims to escape

the rain, watching their mouths move
with words that make no sense to us,
watching their lean pale faces and

the crutches of the lame who'll walk
the hill outside of town to the Mount
of the Beatitudes and be blessed

by the priests. Later, in Capernaum
peddlers hawk postcards, "two for a dollar"
at the synagogue where Jesus taught

as a child. Multitudes gather. Multitudes
walk the hill to the place where Jesus
stood and spoke the Sermon on the Mount.

I stand amazed, mouth open, to see
so many here. The field is full of folk
and flowers. The lame lie down in the long

grass, and Jesus speaks to them. From
over the water he comes and stands
and speaks. Down below the buses belch

diesel smoke and wait.

Oedipus: at the Place Where Three Roads Meet

At the place where three roads meet
Oedipus stops. He has walked from Delphi,
he has walked up the Sacred Way
from the gurgling spring to the space
where the Sybil waits with answers
to the questions of our lives.

Now he knows, now he has heard
her words, and he turns toward Corinth—
no, toward Thebes—to charm his fate
to death, to laugh his destiny
into the black hole where snakes
of superstition dwell. He will smile
at the Sphinx, scoff at the old man
who blocks his way, and place his tongue
in the mouth of the woman he loves.

He will be king. He will give laws.

At the place where three roads meet
he looks down the road to Thebes
and does not see the silver brooches
from his mother's gown tearing, tearing
at the circles of his all knowing eyes.

Behind him, on Parnassus, wild flowers
bloom, and the muses weep silently.

Dodona: Sunday Morning

It is Sunday morning, and I am sitting alone
on the stone steps of the theatre of Dodona.
It is Sunday morning, and to the east the rays
of the sun touch the sacred ground of the oracle
of Zeus. It is a Sunday morning in April
and wild flowers, red and yellow, have begun
to bloom in the wet grass. To the south the high
peaks of the Pindus range are white from last
night's snow. It is April, and the flowers
are blooming, yet the high mountains are white.

The voice of Zeus rolled once from these hills
through the mouths of the sibyls. The drunken
mouths of the sibyls who had breathed the fumes
of the sacred springs. Those who sat on these steps
saw his eagle circling over the distant snow-capped
hills. Now it is Sunday morning, and I have climbed
over the tourist gate to sit here alone while
the April sun rises over the eastern ridge.

The ticket office is closed, the buses have departed,
and the first taxis of the day have not yet made
the winding drive from the valley below. No sign
of life except my footprints in the dew, and the
sun slanting through ancient columns, and the eagle
of Zeus soaring from the snow-capped hills. It is
Sunday morning and I am sitting, alone, on the stone
steps of the theatre of Dodona near the oracle of Zeus.

This Monster Time

From Masaccio's "Expulsion"

This is the moment time begins.
Before—nothing but playing in the
dimpled shade—some milk and honey
dream of endless love. Now there is time.

No one had quite caught it in paint
like Ugly Tom, who must have felt
himself the pain and seen it on
the faces of his friends. Nothing

ideal here. No nudes here. Nothing
gentle or genteel. Just nakedness,
pure nakedness forked out before us.
And the horror in Eve's eyes of the

history that will start unreeling
here forever—Dresden, Auschwitz,
Hiroshima. Adam's guilt hidden
in his hands. Better not to see.

I thought once Eve was modest, now
I know she's only cold and sick, sick
of what they've made and unmade.
Sick at the gurgle of blood in her

son's throat and husband's too,
sick at the sight of her distant
daughters on the road to Beirut
chilled in their black chadours.

Time begins here with these steps,
Adam's right leg dragging at the gate,
Eve's belly swelling. This night
they will sleep in some hollow

and chew on reeds. He will hold her
in his arms, but their eyes will
never meet and they will wonder how
this unravelling began—this monster time.

Come Lord Jesus

from Bernini's "The Ecstasy of St. Teresa"

At the Piazza della Republica I see the gypsy
girls, one coming at me from the front with the
big sheet of cardboard, the other circling behind.
"Via! Via!" I say in Italian, having had the trick
described to me. I cross away from them, looking
for the Largo San Susanna, looking for the Church
of Santa Maria della Vittoria. No one has heard
of it. I have come to see "The Ecstasy
of St. Teresa," but no one knows where it is.

I stand at the top of Via Barberini, showing
my paper to passers by. They shake their heads
and go. Go home, they seem to say, don't worry.
But I do. I have seen the slides in art class
and felt my breath catch even at the pictures.
I have carried the paper with the name of the place
written in Italian so all can understand.
This is my day to see Bernini's "Ecstasy."

I find it by checking churches. There are
four within the block, and the one I seek's
the last of course, covered in scaffolding
and offering nothing at the door except
an invitation to darkness inside, the usual
candles and second-rate baroque. No wonder
the guide books leave it out, I think. And then
I catch it with the corner of my eye and pray
to be alone awhile to let it play on me.

Wherever she is going, she is already there.
"Come Lord Jesus," she says with her open mouth.
Her lidded eyes have slowly closed. Her hand

with its delicate long fingers hangs limply
from the rock where she lies. Her foot falls
loosely into our space. She is one with God.

"Come, Lord Jesus" she has said, and we know
at once the angel is superfluous, the silly
smiling angel, his spear about to pierce
her heart. She has traveled far beyond

his thrust and the leering eyes of the
carved nobles in the boxes on either side
who gaze at her erotically. They cannot find
her. I don't know what the angel thinks.
He's just a boy who's never used a spear
like this before. What I'd like, though,
is the angel's view. He sees her whole
as I cannot, bound to earth as I am.

Later, the schoolgirls come, giggling
while their teacher talks, whispering
to one another of some obscenity they see.
I close my book and leave by the other
aisle. On the street outside the gypsies
ply their trade in the late summer sun.

FROM
THE MAN WHO

2005

The Man Who Feels The Sleeves Of The Snow

On the day after the snow
he takes his usual walk.
The trees
reach out to him.
Their silver sleeves
have no history
no memory of grief.
Their long white fingers know only
the sweet silence
of now.

The Man Who Loved Music

carried his violin to the Armory near ground zero.
He was from Julliard, where music was his life,
where playing better than the next musician
was more important than food, more important
than God.

On the walls of the armory
he saw posters, thousands of posters, the faces
of the missing smiling at him. They were all
young. Maria Ramirez looked out from her
graduation robes. He saw the face of Angela
Susan Perez from the 101st floor of Tower B.
He saw Joe Visciano and Carol Rabalais,
and Paul Ortiz, Jr. holding his baby.

How could music
help in a time like this, he wondered, as he walked
with his violin into the huge central room.
He and his two friends played for hours.
When his friends could play no more,
he played alone. He played for the grief
counselors, for firemen and cops who came in
to rest, and for the soldiers of the Fighting
Sixty-Ninth.

He played Bach and Tchaikovsky,
he played Dvorak and Vivaldi, the theme from
Schindler's List and "Memory" from *Cats*.
For the soldiers who had been "in the pit"
he played "Amazing Grace" and then at
midnight he played the National Anthem
as the three-hundred men of the 69th
stood and saluted an invisible flag.

His hands trembled as he placed his violin
and its bow back in the black case. The colonel
walked him into the dark street, where dust
still thickened the air and faces of the missing
still smiled against the night. He would walk home
and the blisters on his hands would be his remembrance.

The Man Who Forgot His Oil

And the foolish said unto the wise, "Give us of your oil; for
our lamps are gone out." But the wise answered, saying, "Not so,
lest there not be enough for us and you, but go rather to them that sell,
and buy for yourselves."
—Matthew 25: 8-9

We all know the rest of the story, how the foolish
virgins go off to buy oil and miss the wedding.
I can see their faces when they get back, their sad
eyes bent to the ground, their fingers clutching
the jars of now useless oil, the wise ones
smirking, "I told you so," the bride and groom
gone. They sit in the dust and cry. The moral

is obvious. Be prepared. That's the Boy Scout
marching song (thank you, Tom Lehrer). Be
prepared and you'll get into heaven. Good old
Ben Franklin—the early bird gets the worm.
We know all that. But wait just a minute.

This, after all, is the Bible. These are the words
of Jesus—not some practical guide to modern
living. Jesus said, "Love your neighbor." Jesus
said, "He who loses his life for my sake..."
Jesus said, "Feed the hungry, visit the sick..."

But these wise virgins. They're not going
to share. I thought sharing was Christian.
"Go get your own," the wise virgins say.
"You're not using any of my oil." They're
like the older brother in the prodigal son
story who says, "You never gave me a party!"

Hell, I forget my oil all the time. Oil is
a metaphor anyway. Replace "oil" with—
the ATM card, the checkbook, my password—
"whatever" as college students like to say.

And besides, in the story, it's midnight.
I never could figure that one out. I mean,
are stores open at midnight? This is
ancient Palestine. No twenty-four hour
Wal-Marts in those days. So—feed the poor,

visit the sick, love your neighbor, but
for God's sake, don't share your oil.
That's what the Bible says. Help me,
you Bible lovers. Couldn't I share
just a little? Those foolish virgins—they were
much cuter than the wise ones, anyway.

The Man Who Loved Mondays

scratched a living in the briarpatch
for forty years or more. "Oh, it's Monday,"
his colleagues moaned with long mouths.

"Don't throw me in the briarpatch,"
he'd say to himself, curling his hands
like Brer Rabbit's paws. Monday morning

he sat at his desk, sheer joy crinkling
in his eyes, lectures to write, books
to read, students to talk to long

into the lazy afternoons of fall,
the crisp mornings of winter,
when his boots would crunch the first

footprints into the new snow,
into the soft mornings of spring
when the yellow forsythia came

and then the burst of the azaleas
pink and white below his high
window. These days forever coming

Monday after glorious Monday
where the blessed thorns make the blood
run and the quick brain and the turtle

of the heart play catch with the fast
imagination. Now he sits on the shore
and fishes with the arid plain before

and behind. "Catch anything?" the tourists
ask, faces glowing with ghostly screens
against the sun. His bucket is empty.

The Man Who Writes With His Eyes
for Joe Martin

The man who writes with his eyes
blinks the letters into existence.
He creates from nothing.

He's carried on the jet by willing
hands. "Does he understand *anything?*"
a moist-eyed lady asks. "Everything,"

his wife answers, and she is right.
His eyes *see* even the small lines
around our mouths that speak

of who we are. On the ship, curiosity
seekers ask if he is Stephen Hawking.
He could be. He has the same eerie wisdom.

In St. Petersburg at the Hermitage
Museum, he finds a ramp for wheelchairs.
The guards refuse admittance.

"This entrance is for Czars and Heads
of State," they say with grave authority.
He smiles by raising his eyebrows.

They motor to the front, and his lovely
limber men lift him, carry him up
the stairs to the startled gaze of Russian

passers-by. They place him in a chair,
his wife beside him, then return
to haul the three hundred pound

wheelchair up the grudging stones.
Inside he sees the white dining room
where Bolsheviks stopped time

and the thin gold leaf on ornate
painted ceilings. He sees the Prodigal
of Rembrandt, the son held by the

father's loving hands. At the end,
when they bump the wheelchair
down again, the guards salute

in admiration. Later, he will see
Stockholm, Helsinki and Copenhagen
and he will write with his eyes

of their many wonders. But most
he will remember how at the Hermitage
they hauled him up the slow stones,

how he froze in wonder at the peacock
in the glassed in clock and the father
bringing the Prodigal home at last.

The Man Who Loved Animals

July Fourth, early evening, family
and friends gathered, sun setting, fireworks
an hour away, the dog not in his
accustomed place beneath their feet.
They find him in the woods, half buried, surely gone
to die.

Surprisingly the doctor's office answers.
A young vet sewing up a cat says, "Bring
him in" and all of them carry the dying
dog to the waiting van. The doctor
operates at once, and the dog lives
for five more years.

Now, another July morning, Southern sky
hazy blue, the doctor drives to work, son
and heir in his infant chair, facing backwards
as the law prescribes. In his mind he drops
the baby at the sitter, then drives to work,
his brain churning with the day's events:
surgery on an old dog's eye, an evening
meeting at the Y.

The car bakes all day in the summer sun.

At five he leaves to retrieve his son.
The boy, he's sure, has played all day,
napped and sucked the bottle willingly
from the woman's careful hands. He finds
the child silent as a doll.

Over and over his broken heart replays
the morning's ride. He knows he dropped
the baby off.

              So what can we say
of this man who loves the red ears of foxes,
the padded paws of long-legged dogs,
and the soft fingers of his infant son?
That God loved him, loves him still, even after
he has lost all hope of love—that light creeps in
after darkness even when we think
it never can. I know nothing about walking
into light, not even how to take the first step.
But the god who numbers the small bones
in the sparrow's wing can take the fingers
and the light and shape them into something
new.
        This I know and he, I think, knows too.

The Man Who's Forgiven By His Granddaughter
for Clara

Four years old, Clara stands, hands
on hips, eyes fixed on her image
in the glass, then lifts a slippered toe.

She turns to him, flipping her pink
boa across her neck with a gesture
so pure it must have been learned

in another life, then spins away,
skirt aswirl. She leaps and pirouettes,
lost in her storied dreams of silk

and satin and violins. For a second
she holds his gaze as he stands
in the door, watching.

Earlier in the day she had talked
to her mother on the phone.
At the end, she said, "Would you

like to speak with your very
handsome husband?" He had laughed
at the beauty and surprise

of the moment, but she was
disconsolate, inconsolable. She cried
and cursed him for his thoughtlessness.

But now he is forgiven. She dances on,
lost in the rhythm of her painted dream:
she is Snow White, Cinderella at the ball.

Her right hand points toward him
her left slyly lifts a lock of hair—
and she is off again, all fire and air.

The Man Who Hated Teletubbies
for Josie

watched once again with his two-year-old
granddaughter. Perhaps, this time, it would be
better. But no sooner had the four cuddly
blimps appeared, he knew it wouldn't work.

These four parentless creatures of dubious
sex were incapable of any useful activity.
Their range of emotions so narrow that all
feeling was summarized in the universal
word-"oh oh." Tubbie toast flies, bounces
off the walls of their underground hutch,
crumbling on the floor like innumerable bugs.
"oh oh." Tubbie custard flies from its source,
turning the floor to slippery mush. "oh oh."
No worry—Nu Nu, the maternal vacuum
of all trades will clean it up.

                                   They can play
outside and look at bunny rabbits, or perhaps
indulge in a communal hug. Purple
Tinky-Winky, green Dipsy, yellow Lala,
and tiny red Po reach around each others'
shoulders and laugh. But wait! Something
is amiss. Someone has forgotten her,
or is it his, purse. Goodness gracious!
How the plot thickens. Another has left
behind his, or is it her, hat. My, my!

The granddaughter laughs, and repeats
the names. "Po," she says, and "Lala,"
her favorite. And the man who hates
Teletubbies is charmed by the silver
sound of her simple delight.

The Man Who Fears Death
Contemplates The Future

Some days he thinks of extinction.
The cat will walk over his grave
curl its tail and disappear. The sun
will shine despite his lying in the ground.

Other days he runs crying toward
the old man they call God,
wraps his arms around the bony
knees and asks forgiveness.

He loves the stories. Abraham
in the dusty field outside the tent
seeing the three strangers—inside
Sarah laughing—*God can do anything!*

Give an old lady a child, or a virgin
or us, even us, life everlasting.
He loves the stories—the prodigal
muddy and stinking, running,

running toward the father, and then
the same knees, the same knees.
He knows and then he doesn't.
The bombs, the bombs, the bombs

and his heart fails, and he finds
himself alone in the reluctant
ground like a mole sleeping
in February under the snow.

Sleeping with no dreams—
and then Jesus again, touching
the child to life. "Rise," he says,
and the girl's eyes open.

The Man Who Could Not Remember

Catherine Drew Gilpin was nine in 1957.
The man who could not remember was 22.
She was a Girl Scout in Boyce, Virginia.
He was a senior at Princeton University.

On Lincoln's Birthday she wrote to President
Eisenhower in block letters: "I AM NINE YEARS
OLD AND I AM WHITE BUT I HAVE MANY
FEELINGS ABOUT SEGREGATION. WHY SHOULD PEOPLE

FEEL THAT WAY BECAUSE THE COLOR OF THE SKIN?
IF I PAINTED MY FACE BLACK I WOULDN'T BE LET
IN ANY PUBLIC SCHOOLS, ETC. MY FEELINGS
HAVEN'T CHANGED, JUST THE COLOR OF MY SKIN.

LONG AGO ON CHRISTMAS DAY JESUS CHRIST
WAS BORN. AS YOU REMEMBER HE WAS BORN
TO SAVE THE WORLD. NOT ONLY WHITE PEOPLE
BUT BLACK YELLOW RED AND BROWN."

The man read her words in his Alumni Magazine
with great wonder. He studied the block letters
and the lined, three-hole notebook paper. He was
astonished. He saw her looking frankly at the camera

in her Girl Scout uniform, a shelf behind her where
a box of Crayola crayons and a needlepoint kit lay
innocently enough. No signs of radicalism here.
Yet she had written, "COLORED PEOPLE AREN'T

GIVEN A CHANCE.... SO WHAT IF THEIR SKIN
IS BLACK? THEY STILL HAVE FEELINGS BUT
MOST OF ALL ARE GOD'S PEOPLE." Except for
"sincerly" at the end, there were no spelling errors.

The man was nine in 1944, sent off to boarding school
because his home was breaking up. He remembered
riding on the train from New York with the other boys
and watching the black people in the street and in

the windows of apartment buildings when the train
stopped at 125th Street. Surely he could not
have written such a letter as Drew Gilpin's.
He envied the girl her courage and her vision.

Even in 1957 when he was twenty-two
He would not have written to President Eisenhower
He was hard at work in the basement
of the college library on his senior thesis.

He wished to attend graduate school,
and where Rosa Parks sat or did not sit
on a bus in Montgomery, Alabama,
did not concern him.

Now he gazes in awe at the picture
of Drew Gilpin in her Girl Scout uniform,
at her words in their clean block letters.
Her courage burns in his heart.

The Man Whose Mother Was A Boy

"When I was a boy," my mother used to say.
It made me wild. "You can't be a boy,"
I would scream in a very un-boy way.
"Oh yes," she said, "I was a boy before
I became a girl." "Nooo," I cried plaintively,
deceived, depressed, denied the logic
of my simple boy's mind.

                    "When I was a little boy,"
my mother said, "I climbed trees and ran
away from home one night under the Georgia stars.
They found me in a barn and turned me
into a girl so I couldn't escape
anymore. Then I wore dresses and learned
to smile."

Sometimes I became confused and
cried, "My mother was a bird, my mother
was a bird." "Indeed she was," my grandmother
said. "She was a bird, indeed."

Maybe it was she who flew over the house
the other day, and across the lake, diving
to the east, then rising and picking up speed
until she disappeared.

The Man Who Speaks To His Daughter On Her 40th Birthday
May 8, 2003

1.

"Poetry is the supreme fiction," says Wallace Stevens.
I know. Then how to express the truth, simple
and unadorned as Stevens's "dresser of deal."

You see, I am already equivocating, ducking
behind the decoration of language. So, stop me.
Good. That's better. Now, tell me where you are.

If that's too hard, just tell me—something.
Or appear to me in a dream, or leave a symbol somewhere—
some mysterious talisman that lets me know it's you.

Not the feather floating down trick, that's too common.
Nor bumping around in the old house. Something original
like your name spelled in shells before the tide comes in.

2.

All right, let me try it another way. When you were
three, I let you go to school in the winter without
leggings, without anything to warm your legs.

The teacher told me at the end of the day and
I burned with shame. You were my favorite person;
I was yours. And what I really want to know—

now that all the nonsense about your ghostly reappearance
is out of the way—what I really want to know is
where we would have gone, you and I. I want

to think of you at fourteen or twenty-four
or even thirty-one, want to picture you, know
the clothes you would have worn and how

you would have cut your hair. Early this morning
I walked in the rain to your grave. The tree is gone.
You know I picked the spot because the tree

was there, and now it's vanished like my images
of you. Damn it, anyway. I'm supposed to be
a writer, supposed to create you at twenty-five

or thirty-nine, give you a history. What would
you like? A husband, three children of your own?
A law practice in the suburbs of Boston?

3.

I'm such a romantic fool. That's the problem.
The way I see it, I'm sitting in a tea room
in London, it's raining, of course it's raining.

Umbrella stand inside the door. Dripping coats
hanging on the wall. My hands cupped around
a hot mug of tea. I'm breathing steam. I look up.

There you are, at forty, looking at me with so
much love I feel my body rising from the floor.
You walk over. I try to stand. "No," you say,

"Sit down and rest." You place your hands
on my head and tell me all the years were
nothing—a grain of sand, one grain of sand—

that's all. You tell me you'll come for me
whenever it's right, and then you're gone.
The bell rings, door closes, flash of a heel

and then, nothing but the steady fall of rain.
They look at me, there in the shop, all of them,
and then I laugh and cry, too, I'm sure.

Pretty improbable, don't you think? Wouldn't
sell even in Hollywood, or would it? Still,
dammit, I wish you'd talk to me.

Author's Note

Allison Elrod's fresh perspective was invaluable in the selection, arrangement and revision of the poems for inclusion in this book. Leslie Rindoks, my talented editor at Lorimer Press, also designed the book's cover and its content. Nancy Randazzo, Davidson College English Department Assistant, generously contributed her many skills throughout the project. I am very grateful to each of them for their help in the creation of this book.

Anthony Abbott is the author of four volumes of poetry, including the Pulitzer nominated *The Girl in the Yellow Raincoat* and *The Man Who*, winner of the Oscar Arnold Young Poetry Prize. He is also the author of two novels, the Novello Prize winning *Leaving Maggie Hope* and its sequel *The Three Great Secret Things*. A native of San Francisco, he received his undergraduate degree from Princeton University and his Ph.D from Harvard University. He taught for many years at Davidson College, where he is the Charles A. Dana Professor Emeritus of English. He serves as the President of the North Carolina Poetry Society.